FLUTTER

A Colorful Journey with Alphabet Butterflies

By: Jessica Fischer

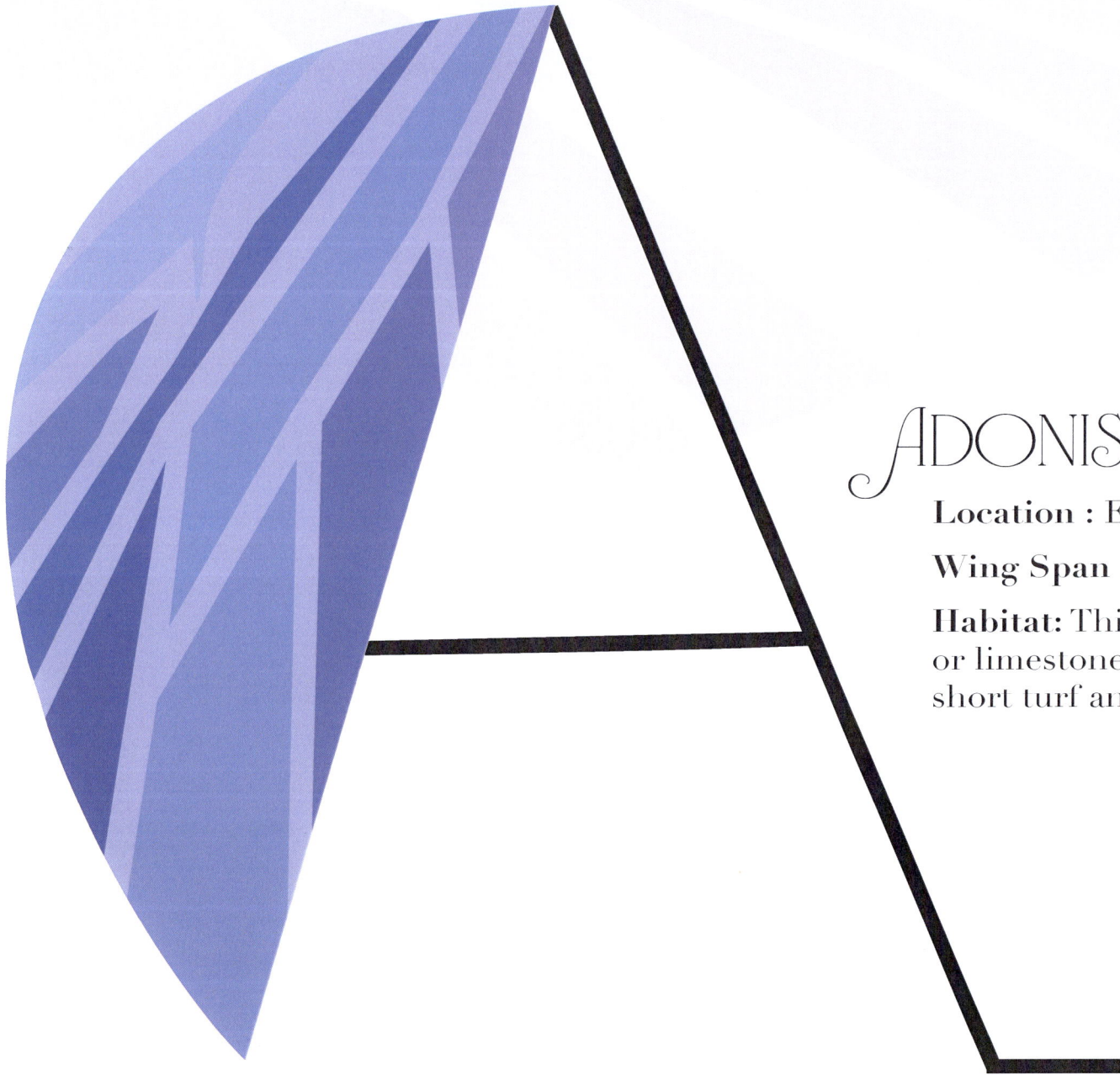

ADONIS BLUE

Location : England

Wing Span : 38mm

Habitat: This butterfly thrives in
or limestone grasslands character
short turf and an abundance of f

BRIMSTONE

Location : England, Wales

Wing Span : 60 mm

Habitat: This butterfly is commonly found in scrubby grasslands and woodlands. It has a wide range and can often be spotted gracefully flying along roadside verges and hedgerows.

COMMON BLUE

Location : Britain and Ireland

Wing Span : 35mm

Habitat: This butterfly is incredibly adaptable and can be found in a variety of [h]particularly in sunny sheltered spots. It is k[n]to thrive in diverse environments such as w[a]grounds, disused pits and quarries, golf cou[rse]and even urban areas like cemeteries. Its ab[ility]adapt allows it to flourish in various settings

DUKE OF BURGUNDY

Location : England

Wing Span : 29-32mm

Habitat: This butterfly primarily inhabits two main habitats: chalk and limestone grasslands that provide ample shelter from scrub, slopes, or clearings on ancient woodland sites. These specific environments offer the necessary conditions for the butterfly's survival and are crucial for its presence in nature.

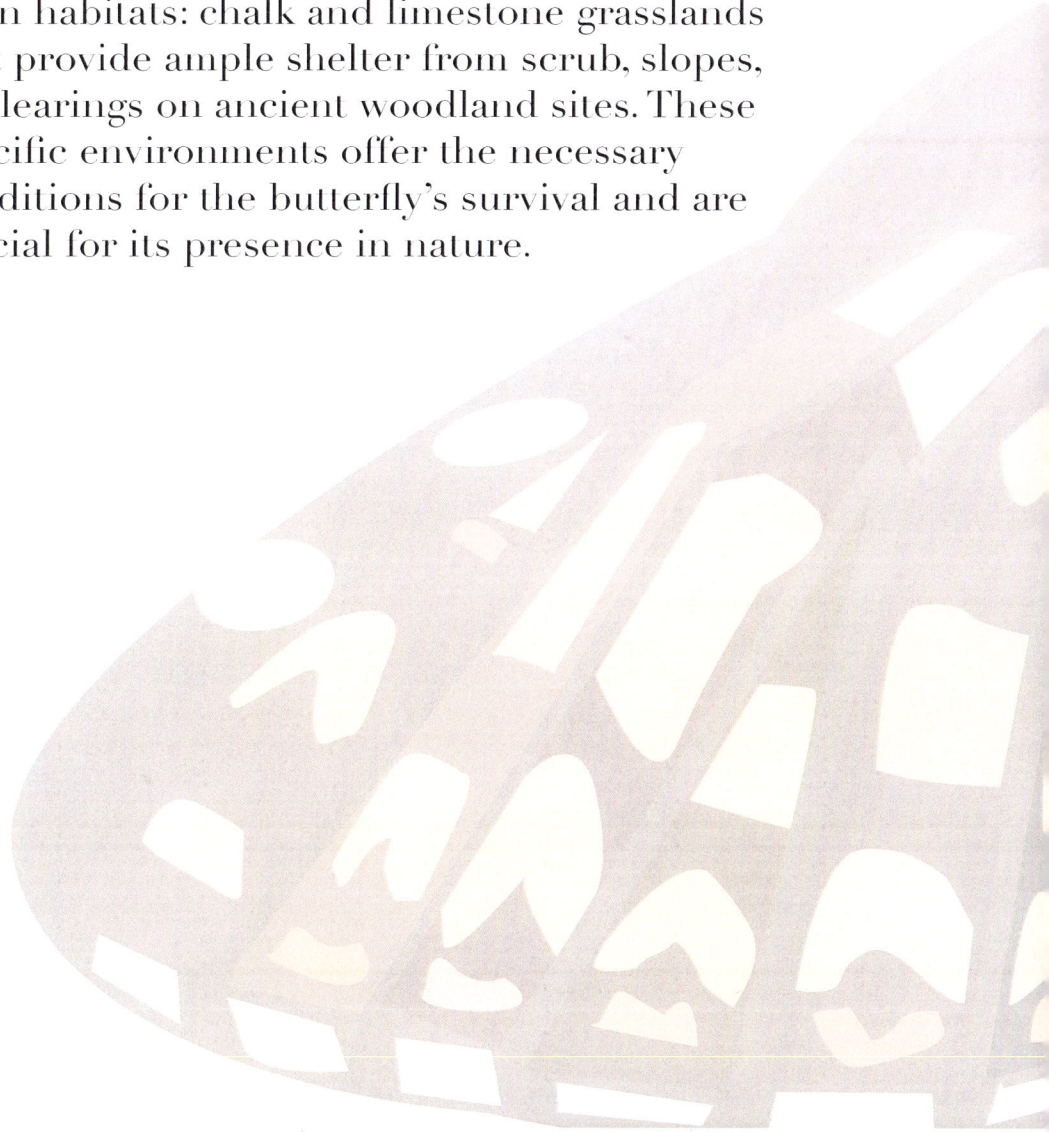

ESSEX SKIPPER

Location : England, Wales

Wing Span : 27-3omm

Habitat: This butterfly is commonly found i
grasslands that are situated in open and su
locations. It can often be spotted along road
woodland rides, and acid grasslands. Additic
known to inhabit coastal marshes. These div
habitats provide the necessary conditions fc
butterfly's survival and contribute to its wid

FOUR-DOTTED ALPINE

Location : United States, Canada

Wing Span : 34-44mm

Habitat: This butterfly is found in the regions of Alaska, western Yukon, and extends eastward into the Northwest Territories, reaching as far as Fort McPherson and Tuktoyaktuk. Its distribution spans across these areas, showcasing its adaptability to different climates within this range.

GREEN – VEINED WHITE

Location : Not specified

Wing Span : 5omm

Habitat: This butterfly exhibits a preference for damp areas characterized by lush vegetation. It can be observed fluttering gracefully in various habitats such as hedgerows, ditches, riverbanks, lakesides, ponds, damp meadows, moorlands, and woodland rides and edges. While it can occasionally be found in gardens, it particularly favors environments with higher moisture levels.

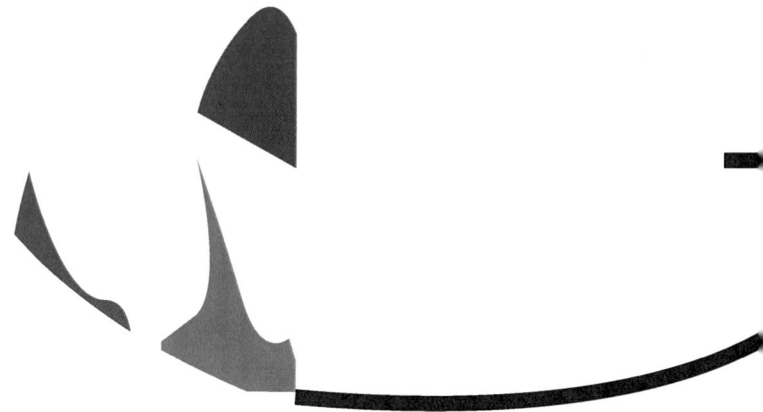

HOLLY BLUE

Location : England, Wales

Wing Span : 35mm

Habitat: This butterfly is a frequent visitor to gardens and can often be spotted in parks, churchyards, hedgerows, and woodlands. Its adaptability allows it to thrive in both urban and natural environments, making it a versatile species that can be enjoyed by nature enthusiasts in various settings.

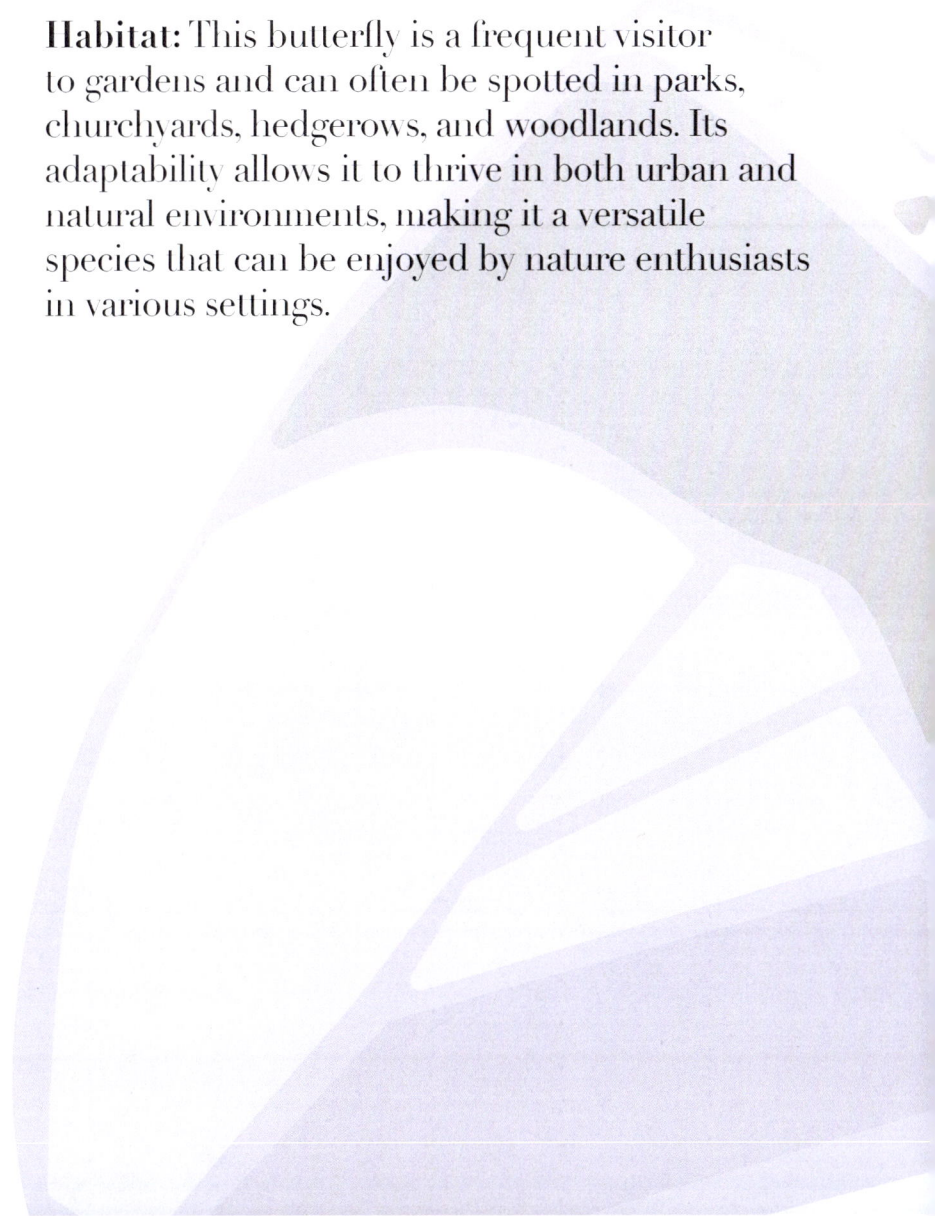

Indra Swallowtail

Location: Canada

Wing Span: 58-72mm

Habitat: This butterfly primarily inhabits dry mountainous areas throughout most of its range. It is well-adapted to these rugged environments and can be commonly found in such regions. Additionally, it has been observed in deserts located farther south, showcasing its ability to tolerate and survive in arid conditions as well.

Johansen's Sulfur

Location: Near Bernard Harbour, Nunavut

Wing Span: 35-38mm

Habitat: This butterfly is restricted to dry steppe-like tundra habitats. It is known for its unique flight pattern, characterized by a distinctive zigzag motion as it flies up and down the hillsides. This behavior sets it apart from other butterflies, including the Hecla Sulphur, even when observed in flight. The specific habitat preference and flight pattern make it easily distinguishable in its natural environment.

KRAUTHS SULPHUR

Location: United States

Wing Span: 35-52mm

Habitat: This butterfly is primarily found in the Black Hills region of South Dakota. The unique characteristics of this area provide a suitable habitat for the butterfly, allowing it to thrive and contribute to the biodiversity of the region.

LARGE COPPER

Location: British Isles

Wing Span: 44-52mm

Habitat The Large Copper butterfly was once found in the fens of East Anglia and potentially other damp areas of southern England. However, sadly, it is now considered extinct in these regions. The loss of its habitat and other factors have contributed to its disappearance from these areas. Efforts to conserve and restore suitable habitats may offer hope for potential reintroduction or population recovery in the future.

MONARCH

Location : United States

Wing Span: 95-100mm

Habitat: While considered a rare mig
UK, in their native home of the Unite
this butterfly can be found in a wide
habitats. They are known to inhabit a
their food plants grow, includi
farmland, gardens, and ev
roadsides. Their adapta
allows them to thrive
environments and
various landscape
sustenance and
opportunities.

Northern Brown Argus

Location: Britain, England

Wing Span: 29mm

Habitat: This butterfly typically occurs in well-drained, lightly grazed, or un-grazed unimproved grasslands. It shows a preference for sheltered habitats that often include scrub and patches of bare ground. Examples of such habitats include sand dunes, quarries, coastal valleys, and steep slopes. These specific environments provide the necessary conditions for the butterfly's survival and are crucial to its presence in nature.

ORANGE – TIP

Location: Not specified

Wing Span: 45-50mm

Habitat: Orange-tips prefer damp habitats such as meadows, woodland glades, hedgerows and the banks of streams and rivers, but readily visit gardens.

EACOCK

 tion: Britain and Ireland

Span: 63-69mm

at: This butterfly is common and
e found in a wide range of habitats.
aptability allows it to thrive in
e environments, including meadows,
ands, gardens, parks, and even
areas. The butterfly's ability to
various habitats contributes to its
pread distribution and presence in
ent ecosystems.

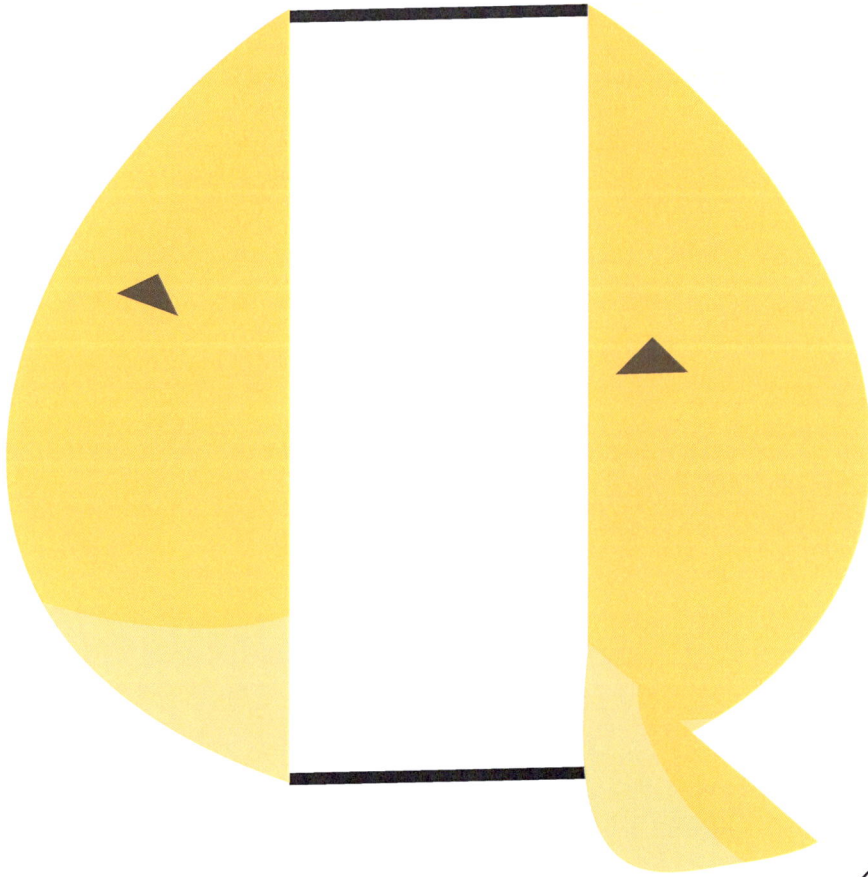

Queen Alexandra's Sulf

Location: Variety

Wing Span: 38-57mm

Habitat: This butterfly is primarily located in the parts of New Mexico and extends into southern Sa southern Alberta, and southern British Columbia. distribution spans across these regions, showcasin adaptability to different climates within this range

Red Admiral

Location: Not specified

Wing Span: 67-72mm

Habitat: This butterfly is incredibly versatile and can be found in almost any habitat. From gardens to sea-shores, town centers to the top of mountains, it has the ability to adapt and thrive in a wide range of environments. Its presence in such diverse habitats highlights its resilience and ability to utilize various resources for survival.

SWALLOWTAIL

Location: England

Wing Span: 80-90mm

Habitat: While this butterfly can be foun
any habitat, it is most frequently observe
areas near the south coast of England. Th
regions provide favorable conditions for
presence and are often where it is comm
However, its adaptability allows it to expl
inhabit various other habitats as well.

Tiger Swallowtail

Location: United States, Canada

Wing Span: 65-90mm

Habitat: This butterfly is found throughout the United States west of the Rocky Mountains. In Canada, it has been recorded primarily in southern British Columbia, ranging from Vancouver Island east through the lower Fraser River Valley and extending north into the Okanagan and Kootenay Valleys. Its distribution in these regions highlights its presence in diverse habitats within this range.

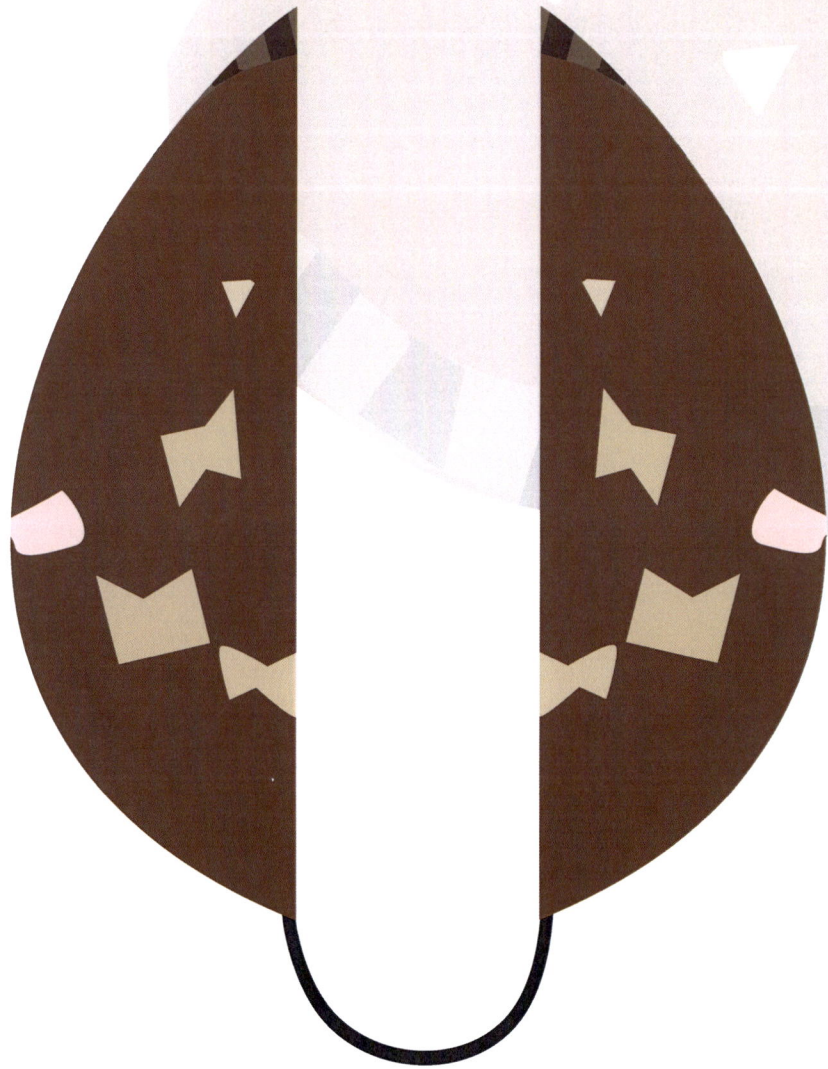

URBANUS PROTEUS

Location: United States, Argentina

Wing Span: 37-46mm

Habitat: This butterfly is a resident species found fr[om]
Argentina to the extreme southern United States. Ho[wever, it]
also migrates northward each summer, occasionally r[eaching]
as far as Michigan. In 1994, there was a notable occur[rence]
of this butterfly in southwestern Ontario, showcasing [its]
ability to expand its range during migration. The but[terfly's]
migratory behavior allows it to explore and inhabit d[iverse]
regions throughout its annual life cycle.

VACCINIINA OPTILETE YUKMA

Location: Variety

Wing Span: 18-24mm

Habitat: This butterfly is found in the Old World, spanning from central Europe to Siberia and Japan. In North America, its range extends from Duck Mountain Provincial Park in Manitoba to northern British Columbia, Nunavut, the Northwest Territories, Yukon, and Alaska. The butterfly's distribution across these regions showcases its ability to thrive in diverse habitats and climates throughout its range.

WHITE ADMIRAL

Location: England, Wales, Britain

Wing Span : 60-64mm

Habitat: This butterfly is commonly found in shady woodlands a[nd] ride edges. It has a strong association with neglected or mature woodland, particularly in areas where there are sunny glades and patches of Bramble that provide nectar for the adults. It can be fo[und] in both deciduous and mixed deciduous/coniferous woodlands, showcasing its adaptability to different types of forested environm[ent.] The specific habitat preferences contribute to the butterfly's surv[ival] and successful reproduction.

XERCES BLUE

Location: United States

Wing Span: 18-28mm

Habitat: Originally, in 1852, this butterfly was endemic to the coastal sand dunes of the upper San Francisco Peninsula. It was once locally common in this region, including sites that are now within the Golden Gate National Recreation Area. The butterfly's presence in these specific areas highlights its historical association with the unique coastal sand dune habitat of the region.

Yellow-Dotted Alpine

Location: United States, Siberia

Wing Span: 29-38mm

Habitat: The Yellow-dotted Alpine butterfly is known to fly throughout a large area of Alaska and Yukon. It also has isolated populations in northern British Columbia, specifically in Stone Mountain Provincial Park, as well as in northern Manitoba (Churchill). In the United States, it can be found in Montana, Wyoming, and Colorado. The butterfly's distribution across these regions showcases its ability to inhabit diverse habitats within its range.

Zarucco Duskywing

Location: United States

Wing Span: 32-38mm

Habitat: The Zarucco Duskywing butterfly is primarily found in the southeastern United States. However, it also exhibits migratory behavior and can be observed migrating northward to Pennsylvania and even as far as Toronto. This migration allows the butterfly to expand its range during certain times of the year, showcasing its ability to adapt and explore different regions within its annual life cycle.

Remember, when searching for butterflies, approach them gently and quietly so as not to startle them away. Observe their delicate patterns and graceful flight as they bring joy wherever they go.

Butterflies are nature's colorful gems—symbols of transformation and beauty that remind us of the wonders all around us!

www.ingramcontent.com/pod-product-compliance
Lightning Source LLC
Chambersburg PA
CBRC101537260326
41914CB00023B/1651